## Class Book 4

**Paul A Davies   Carolyn Graham
Culture Club by Sally McGugan**

Senhores pais,

Bem-vindos ao curso de inglês *Kids United*. Durante o próximo ano escolar seus filhos aprenderão inglês na companhia dos personagens Leo, Laura e Zabadoo. Através destes personagens, seus filhos aprenderão palavras e estruturas básicas da língua inglesa, juntamente com várias canções e chants.

A presença destes personagens ajuda a tornar a linguagem mais viva, motivando as crianças a falar inglês e ajudando-os a compreender e memorizar fatos, frases e palavras. Ao final de cada unidade os alunos farão um trabalho que poderá ser incluído na pasta de trabalhos individuais (*'My Portfolio'*). Peçam a eles que mostrem e expliquem cada um destes trabalhos a vocês para que juntos escolham quais incluir na pasta.

O material fornecido em cada unidade foi elaborado especialmente para motivar as crianças a participar das aulas com entusiasmo, sem pressão excessiva na produção oral, que deve acontecer de forma natural e espontânea. A grande variedade de atividades inclui canções, jogos e dramatizações e tem como principal objetivo envolver as crianças lingüística, mental e fisicamente. Nas seções denominadas *'Culture Club'* são propostas atividades destinadas a aumentar a consciência cultural das crianças através da comparação entre festividades e costumes do Brasil e países de língua inglesa.

Desejamos que seus filhos se divirtam ao aprender inglês com *Kids United*.

Paul A Davies  Carolyn Graham
Os autores

# 1 Animals

**1** Listen and point. Listen and say.

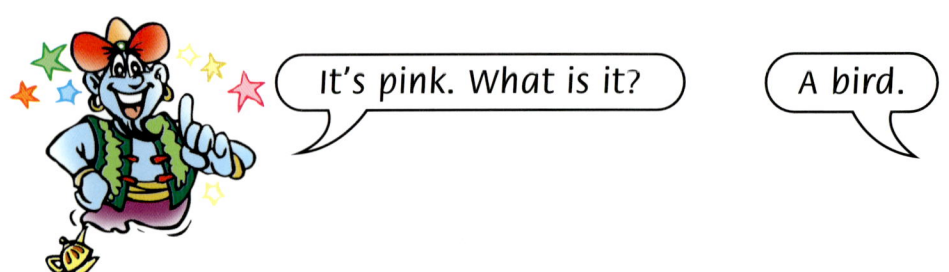

1. an elephant
2. a monkey
3. a lion
4. a zebra
5. a fish
6. a bird

It's pink. What is it?

A bird.

## 2  Say the chant.

I can swim like a fish,
I can jump like a lion,
I can climb like a monkey in a tree.
I can run like a zebra,
I can fly like a bird,
I can walk like an elephant.
Hey! Look at me!

## 3  Listen and point. Then listen and choose.

1. a mouse
2. a rabbit
3. a parrot
4. a fox
5. a dolphin
6. a cat

# Laura's new pet

**5** **Read, match and write. Then color.**

a cat   a fish   a mouse   a parrot   a rabbit

1 This is my pet. It's brown. It has a white tail. It can jump.
_It's a rabbit._

2 This is my pet. It's green and red. It can fly.
It's _____ .

3 This is my pet. It's red. It has a tail. It can swim.
_____ .

4 This is my pet. It's orange and black. It has green eyes. It can run and jump.
_____ .

5 This is my pet. It's white. It has a small pink tail and a pink nose. It's very small.
_____ .

It has a (white) (tail). It can (jump).

**6** Ask your friends. Write.

| Name | Pet? | Favorite animal? |
|---|---|---|
| Hilary | cat | lion |
| Henry | X | elephant |
|  |  |  |
|  |  |  |

**7** Make a picture.

Do you have a pet? Yes, I have a (cat).

**8** **Sing the song.** 🔊 6

Monkeys swing
Up and down,
Monkeys swing
All around.

Monkeys swing,
Tigers bite,
But crocodiles crawl
All night.

Dolphins swim
Up and down,
Dolphins swim
All around.

Dolphins swim,
Tigers bite,
But crocodiles crawl
All night.

Rabbits hop
Up and down,
Rabbits hop
All around.

Rabbits hop,
Tigers bite,
But crocodiles crawl
All night.

# 1  Now I can...

**A** Can you count and write? Now color.

I can see six yellow _____, five brown _____,

four green _____, three black and white _____,

two gray _____, and one pink _____.

**B** Can you do the animal puzzle?

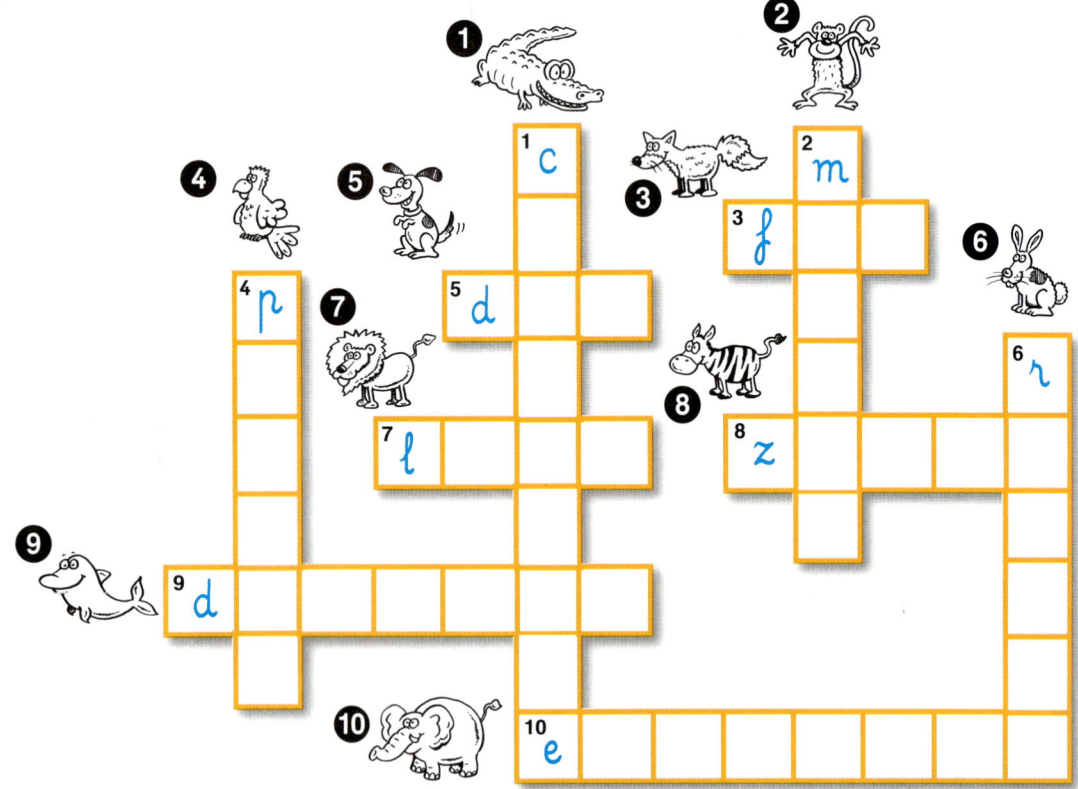

**C** Can you read, write and color?

> a bird   a crocodile   a long tail   wings   can fly   can swim

1

It's _a crocodile_.

It's green.

It has _____

and a big mouth.

It _____.

2

It's _____.

It's black and white. It has

_____.

It _____.

**D** Can you find the mistakes? Now write.

1

It has two legs.

_____.

2

It can swim.

_____.

3

It has a short tail.

_____.

4

It's small.

_____.

# Pets

Culture Club

Cats, dogs and fish are the favorite pets.
Some pets live at school!
Fish, rabbits and hamsters are the favorite school pets.

This is our pet hamster - Harry.

cat   dog   fish   rabbit

**1** Do a survey of pets and favorite names.

**2** Sing the song.

Do your ears hang low?
Do they wobble to and fro?
Can you tie them in a knot?
Can you tie them in a bow?
Can you throw them over
your shoulder
Like a regimental soldier?
Do your ears hang low?

hamster   collar   cage   survey

# 2 Our house

**1** Listen and say the room. Listen and point.

There's a (sofa) in the (living room).

## 2  Say the chant. 🔊11

There's a cat in the cupboard,
There are cats on the floor,
There's a dog on the bookcase,
There are dogs behind the door,
There's a rabbit on the sofa,
There are rabbits on the chair,
There's a mouse under the table,
There are mice in my hair!

## 3  Listen and choose. 🔊12

1

under

2

in

3
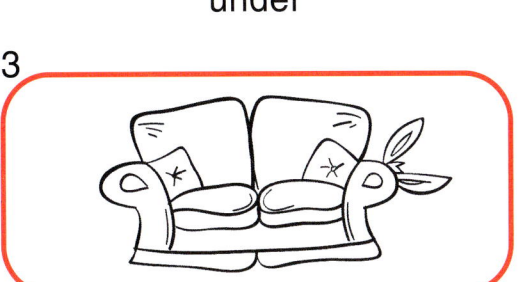
behind

4

on

There's a cat (under) the chair.

**5** **Look and write.**

under   on   in   behind

Where's the skateboard?
*It's under the table.*

Where's the ball?
_____ .

Where's the kite?
_____ .

Where's the guitar?
_____ .

Where's the hat?
_____ .

Where's the bag?
_____ .

**6** **Play the game.**

**Choose five things and hide them in your bedroom.**

My bedroom                          My friend's bedroom

Is there a guitar?

Yes.

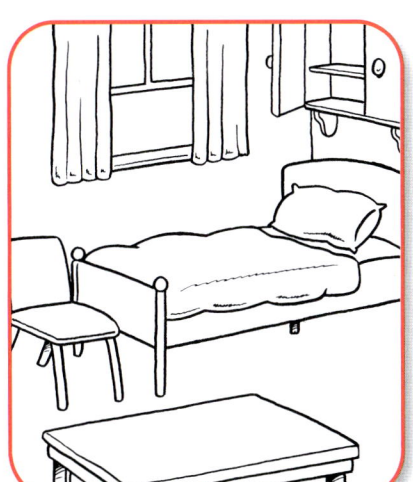

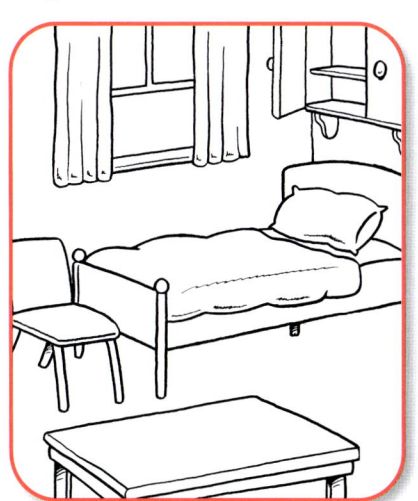

Where's the (skateboard)? It's (under) the table.
Is there a (pen)? Yes. No.

**7** **Sing the song.**

Where do you live?
  I live in a tree house.
Where do you live?
  I live in the sky.
I want to live in a tree house, too.
I don't know why.

I want to live in a tree house.
I want to live in the sky.
I want to live in a tree house, too.
I don't know why.

Where do you live?
  I live in an igloo.
Where do you live?
  I live in the snow.
I want to live in an igloo, too.
Why? I don't know.

I want to live in an igloo.
I want to live in the snow.
I want to live in an igloo, too.
Why? I don't know.

**8** Read, look and choose a or b.

1 There's a yellow chair.  ⓐ  ⓑ
2 There's a white table.   ⓐ  ⓑ
3 There's a black bookcase. ⓐ  ⓑ
4 There's a blue sofa.     ⓐ  ⓑ
5 There's a red sofa.      ⓐ  ⓑ

**9** Make a picture.

# 2

**A** Can you circle and tick?

Look →↓

| | c | c | h | a | i | r | w | s | o | b |
|---|---|---|---|---|---|---|---|---|---|---|
| bath ☐ | x | u | a | e | r | c | b | p | k | o |
| bed ☐ | j | p | b | a | r | r | i | e | k | o |
| bookcase ☐ | d | b | o | d | b | a | t | h | f | k |
| chair ✓ | c | o | s | t | o | v | e | f | r | c |
| stove ☐ | z | a | k | e | d | c | b | b | i | a |
| cupboard ☐ | m | r | c | e | u | o | a | a | d | s |
| fridge ☐ | h | d | a | t | a | b | l | e | g | e |
| sofa ☐ | k | l | s | s | e | e | u | j | e | g |
| table ☐ | b | e | d | y | a | s | o | f | a | f |

**B** Can you look and write?

Where's Henry?

Hilary's Look Out! Machine

1. He's under the table.
2. _____
3. _____
4. _____

# 3 In the park

**1** Listen and point. Listen and answer. 🔊17

1. She's playing tennis.
2. He's drinking.
3. She's eating.
4. She's swimming.
5. He's running.
6. He's riding a bike.

What's Sandy doing?

She's swimming.

What's (Tim) doing? He's (running).

**2** **Say the chant.** 🔊 18

Sandy's in the kitchen,
She's sitting on a box.
Dad's in the bathroom,
He's putting on his socks.
Grandma's in the bedroom,
She's lying on the bed.
Granddad's in the park,
He's standing on his head!

**3** **Listen and number.** 🔊 19

## 5 Look, read and write.

What's Leo doing?
He's lying on the bed.

What's Laura doing?
She's _____.

What's Leo's mom doing?
_____.

What's Tim doing?
_____.

## 6 Listen and point. Then match.

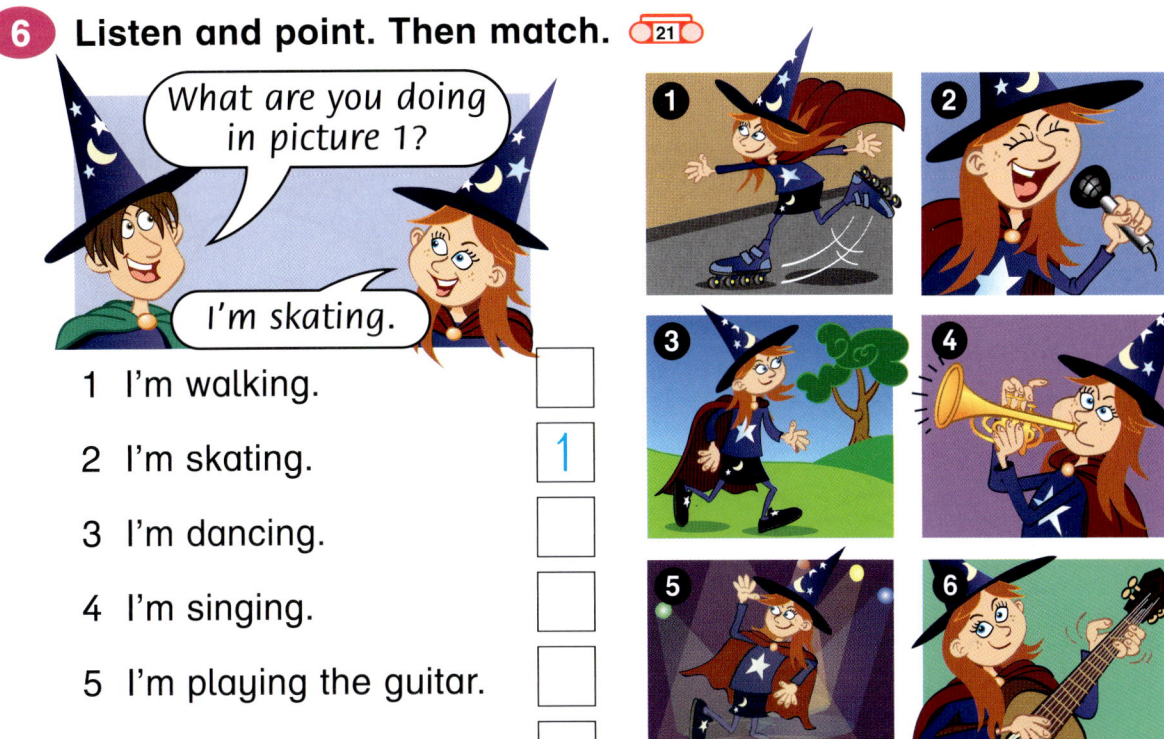

1  I'm walking.  ☐
2  I'm skating.  [1]
3  I'm dancing.  ☐
4  I'm singing.  ☐
5  I'm playing the guitar.  ☐
6  I'm playing the trumpet.  ☐

What are you doing? I'm (skating).

**7** **Sing the song.**

What's the weather like today?
Sunny, it's sunny.
What's the weather like today?
Sunny, it's sunny.
Sunny, it's sunny,
Everyone is smiling.
Sunny, it's sunny,
Everyone is glad.

What's the weather like today?...
Rainy, it's rainy,
Everyone is frowning.
Rainy, it's rainy,
Everyone is sad.

What's the weather like today?...
Snowy, it's snowy,
Everyone is smiling.
Snowy, it's snowy,
Everyone is glad.

What's the weather like today?...
Windy, it's windy,
Everyone is frowning.
Windy, it's windy,
Everyone is sad.

**8** Listen and point. Play the game. 🔊23

It's sunny.   It's rainy.   It's cloudy.   It's windy.

1  2  3  4
5  6  7  8

- What's the weather like?
- It's cloudy.
- What are you doing?
- I'm playing tennis.
- Number 4!

**9** Make a picture about you and your friends.

My Portfolio

It's sunny. I'm playing basketball. Ben's skating. Sally's dancing.   Joe

## 3 The Red Parrot Club

**10**

**1** Dan's wearing the Super Shoes.

Look, there's Vinny.

Wheeee! The Super Shoes are amazing!

**2** He's watching us.

He wants the Super Shoes.

**3** He's running away now. He's scared.

What's this?

**4** It's a treasure map.

There's treasure in the park.

**5** In the park …

Where's the treasure?

It's over there.

# 3

**A** Can you look and write?

What's Henry doing?

Hilary's Look Out! Machine

1. He's running.
2. 
3. 
4. 

**B** Can you do the puzzle?

1. 
2. I'm playing the guitar.
3. 
4.

**C** Can you look and write?

1 It's sunny.  2 _____.
3 _____.  4 _____.

**D** Can you look, read and circle a or b?

1 The boy is running.    Picture **a**    Picture **b**
2 It's sunny.    Picture **a**    Picture **b**
3 The girl is eating.    Picture **a**    Picture **b**
4 It's rainy.    Picture **a**    Picture **b**
5 The boy is skating.    Picture **a**    Picture **b**

# Home

## upstairs

## downstairs

**1** Say the rhyme. 🔊 26

A hive for a honey-bee,
A kennel for a dog,
A hutch for a rabbit,
And a pond for a frog,
A stable for a donkey,
A hole for a mouse ...
But I would like a cabin
For my special house!

**2** Design a special house.

window   porch   cabin   fireplace

# 4 Shopping

**1** Listen and say the number. Listen and answer.

**SHOPPING MALL**

the toy store    the pet store    the sports store
the stationer's    the supermarket    the clothing store

1 THE TOY STORE
2 THE PET STORE
3 THE SPORTS STORE
4 THE STATIONER'S
5 THE SUPERMARKET
6 THE CLOTHING STORE

Where can you buy cheese?

At the supermarket.

**2** **Say the chant.** 28

Look inside the honey jar,
How much money do you have?
Twenty cents, thirty cents,
Forty cents, fifty cents,
Sixty cents, seventy cents,
Eighty cents, ninety cents,
One dollar in the honey jar,
What a lot of money you do have!

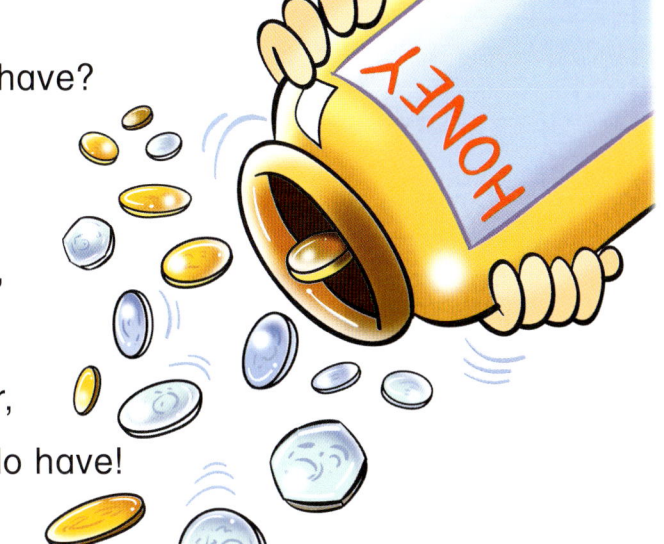

**3** **Listen and repeat. Listen and choose.** 29

twenty-seven cents

thirty-six cents

fifty-one cents

sixty-one cents

one dollar

a hundred dollars

# Mother's Day

**1.** Let's buy some flowers for your mom. — OK. I have $4.

**2.** How much are these flowers? — Five dollars.

**3.** Those flowers are $4.50. Can I borrow 50 cents, please, Laura?

**4.** Of course. Here you are, Leo. — Thanks.

**5.** My mom loves pink flowers.

**6.** My hat! Please, be careful! — Sorry, Mrs. Sharp!

## 5 Draw and write words in the stores.

s _ _ _ _ _ _ _ _ 's

ruler

s _ _ _ _ _ _ _ _ t

cheese

## 6 Listen and act.

A pencil, please.

Hilary's Stationer's

How much is that?

Forty-five cents.

Here you are.

Thank you.

Goodbye.

Goodbye.

How much is that? Forty-five cents.

## 7 Look and write.

"How much money do you have?"

1. I have two dollars fifty cents.

2. I have _____.

3. _____.

4. _____.

## 8 Make a picture.

**My Portfolio**

There's a clothing store in my town.

You can buy jeans, T-shirts and dresses.

Louisa

I have (two) dollars (fifty) cents.

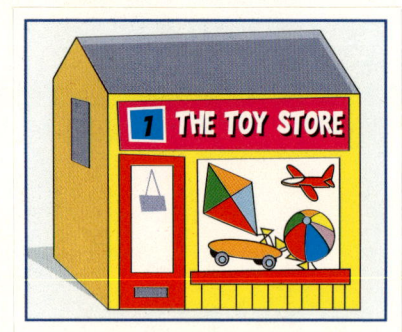

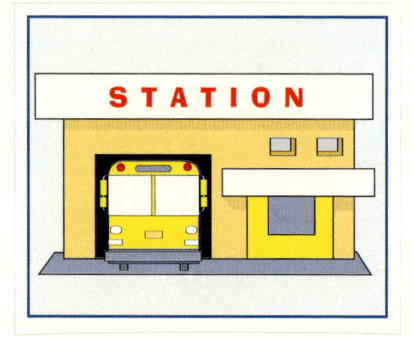

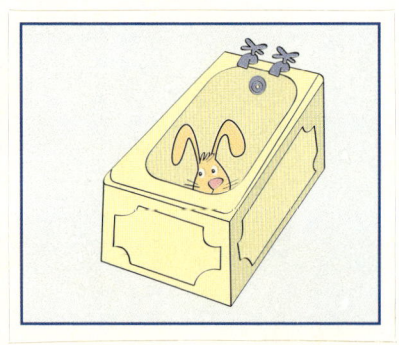

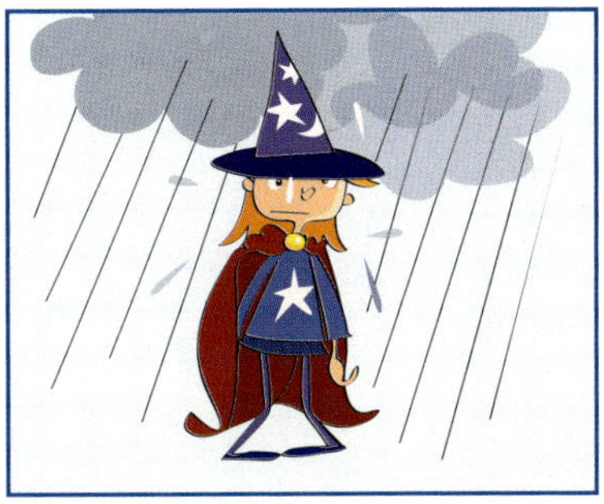

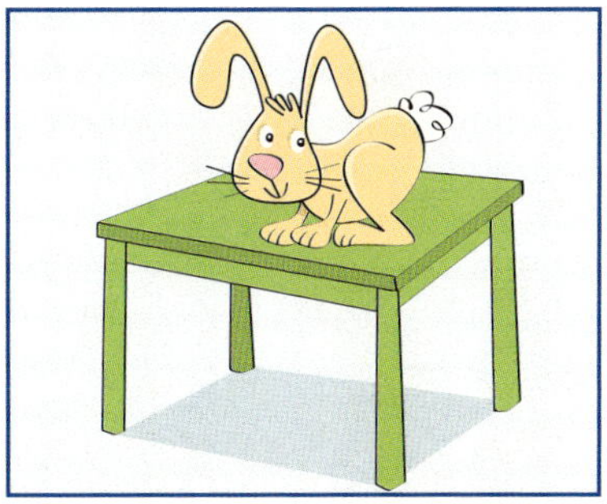

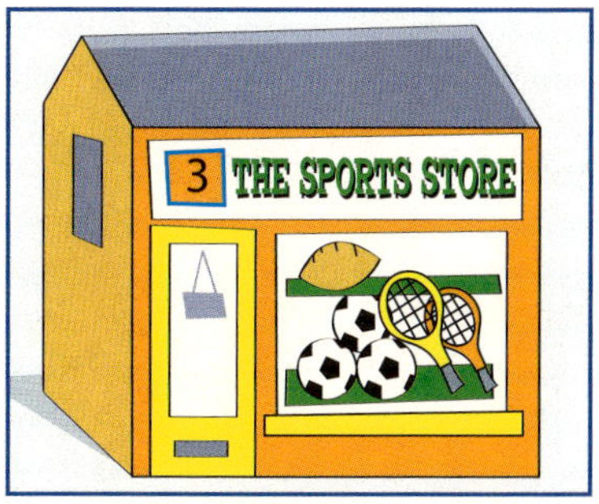
3 THE SPORTS STORE

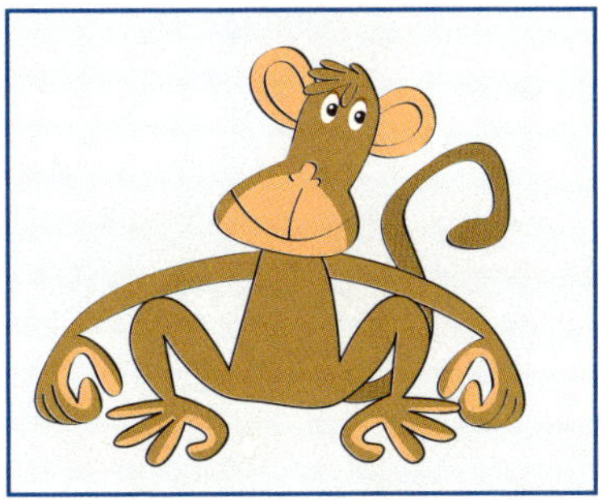

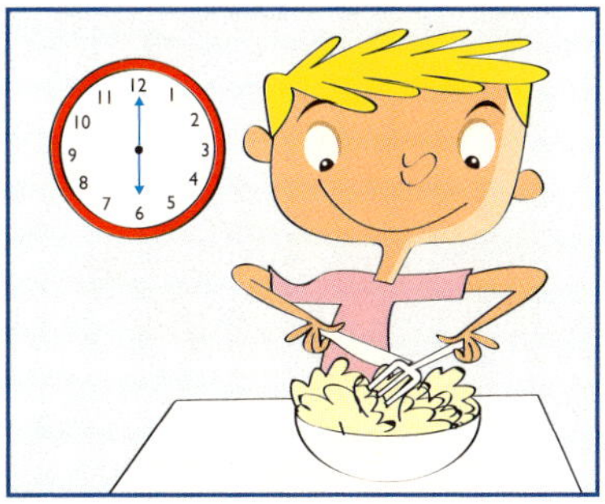
12 1 2 3 4 5 6 7 8 9 10 11

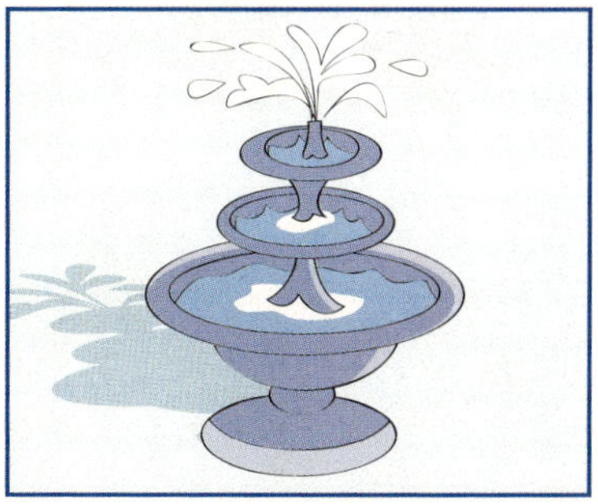

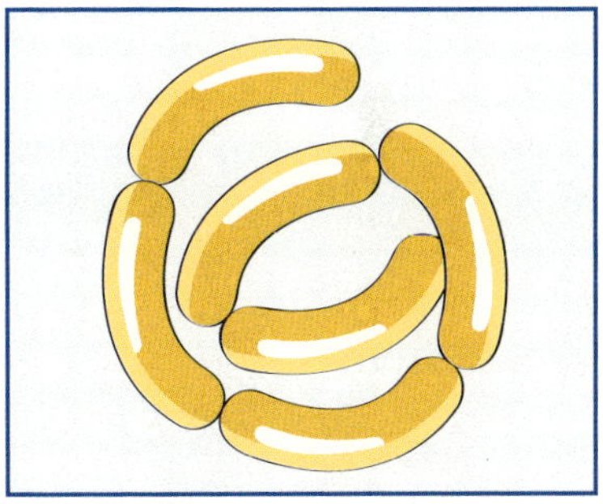

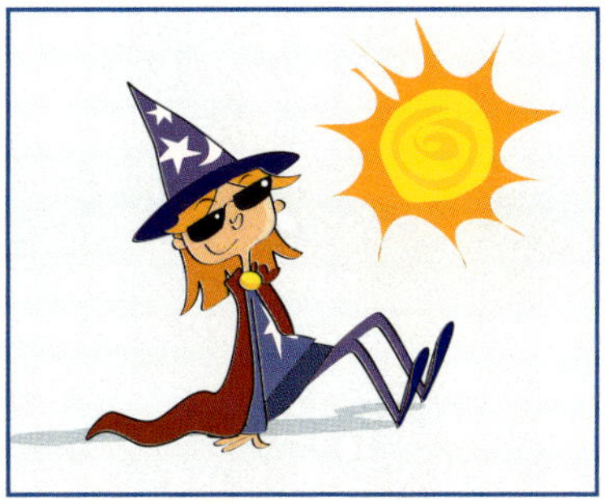

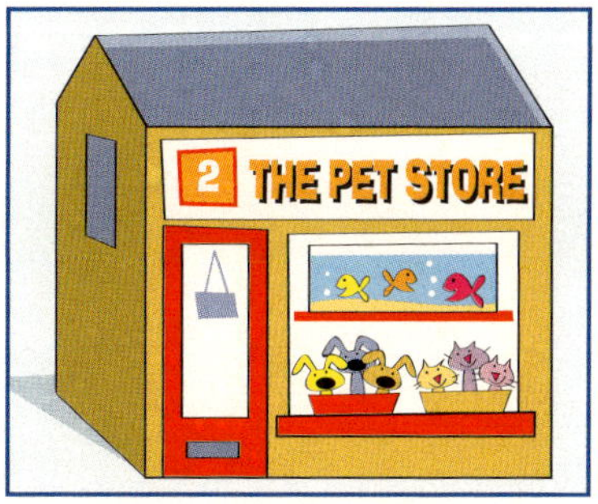
2 THE PET STORE

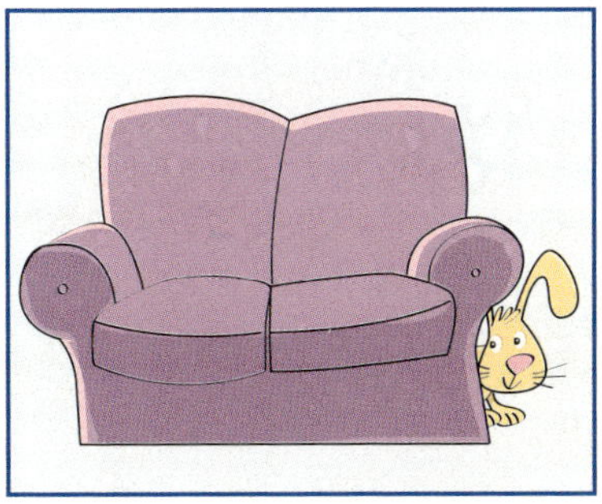

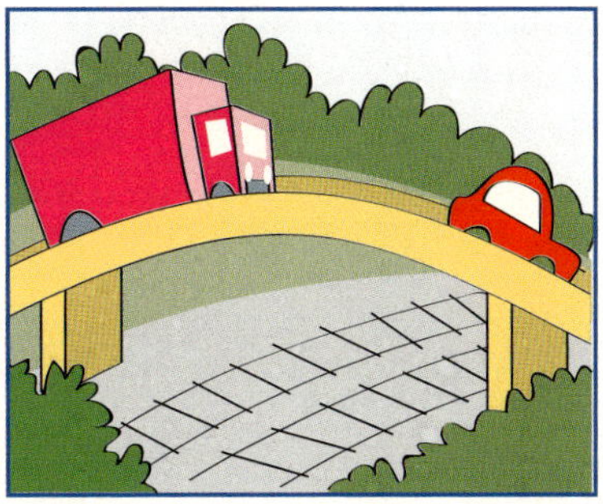

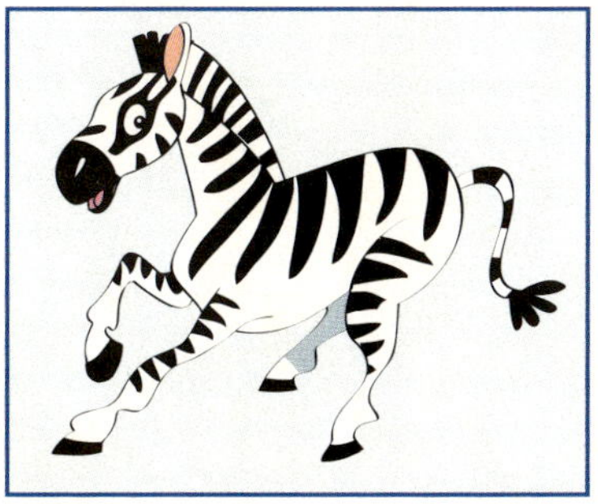

**9  Sing the song.**

He wants to buy an apple,
She wants to buy a pear,
But I want to buy an elephant,
I want to buy a bear.

He wants to buy a table,
She wants to buy a chair,
But I want to buy an elephant,
I want to buy a bear.

A big, brown, beautiful bear,
A big, brown, beautiful bear!

He wants to buy a jacket,
Something warm to wear,
But I want to buy an elephant,
I want to buy a bear.

She wants to buy a little doll,
With long blond curly hair,
But I want to buy an elephant,
I want to buy a bear.

# The Red Parrot Club

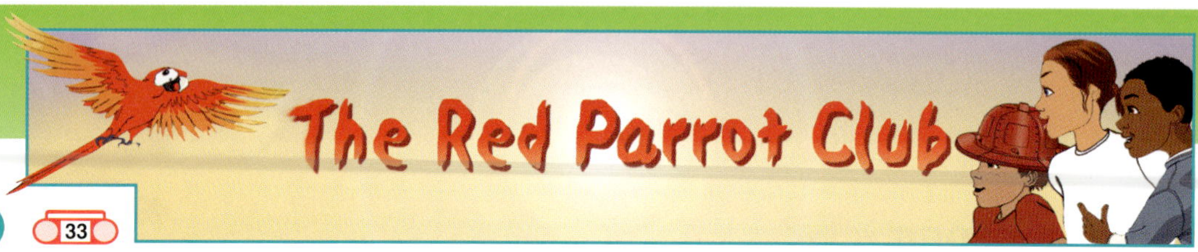

**10**

**1** In a computer store ...
- A webcam, please.
- That's forty dollars.

**2** In a toy store ...
- How much is that balloon?
- Five dollars, please.

**3** At the tree house ...
- A webcam, a balloon ... What are you doing, Fay?
- Shh! Wait and see.

**4**
- Now we can see in the tree house. We can listen, too.
- Great idea, Fay!

**5**
- Are the Super Shoes safe?
- Yes, they're OK.

**6** Look! A secret cupboard!

Aha!

**7** A balloon? What's happening?

**8** POP

**9** Ouch! My ears!

**10** That's strange. What are they doing?

I don't know.

# 4 Now I can...

**A** Can you match and write?

I'm buying a puppet.
*I'm in the toy store.*

I'm buying a pencil.
*I'm in the* _____.

I'm buying a T-shirt.
_____.

I'm buying some rice.
_____.

**B** Can you find the mistakes? Now write.

1 There's a _____ in the _____.
2 There's a _____ in the _____.
3 There's a _____ in the _____.

**C** Can you write the numbers?

*Hilary's Math Machine*

fourteen + seven = _twenty-one_.

twenty + twelve = _____.

thirty + thirty = _____.

ten + forty-five = _____.

fifteen + fifty = _____.

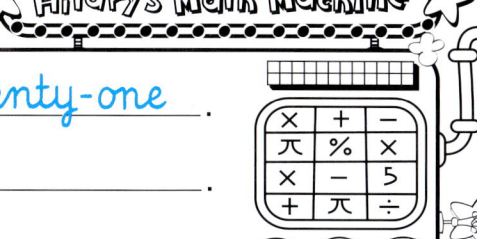

**D** Can you do the puzzle?

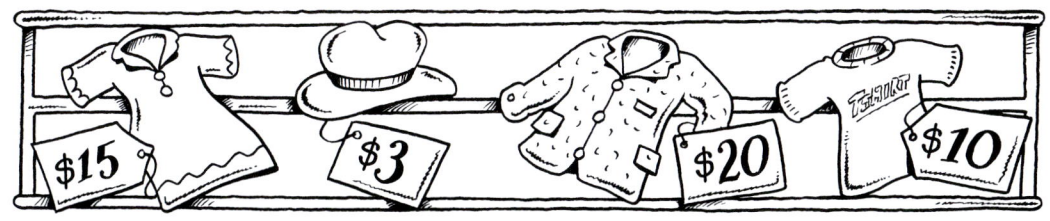

$15   $3   $20   $10

A hat and _a dress_, please.

That's eighteen dollars.

A dress and _____, please.

That's twenty-five dollars.

A hat, a T-shirt and _____, please.

That's thirty-three dollars.

_____ and _____, please.

That's twenty-three dollars.

45

# 5 Meal times

**1** Listen and say the number. Listen and answer. 🔊 35

1. oranges
2. tomatoes
3. sausages
4. sandwiches
5. chips
6. bananas

What's in the cupboard?

Oranges.

**2** Say the chant. 🔊 36

Sausages for breakfast,
Sausages for lunch,
Sausages for dinner,
Munch, munch, munch.
I don't like carrots,
And I don't like peas,
But I LOVE sausages,
Sausages, please!

**3** Listen and circle a or b. 🔊 37

1  a  (b)     2  a  b     3  a  b
4  a  b      5  a  b     6  a  b

# 5 Sandy's breakfast

**4** 🔊 38

**1** What time is it?
It's eight o'clock. I'm late! Can you feed Sandy, please?

**2** Sandy loves sausages.
The sausages are for me. Sandy's food is in the cupboard.

**3** Hmm. Cereal, orange juice … Can you help me, please, Dad?
OK.

**4** Here's Sandy's food. It's behind the cereal.
Thank you.

**5** Where's Sandy?
And where are my sausages?

**6** Bad dog, Sandy!

**5** Listen. Draw and write the times.

1. It's seven o'clock.
2. It's _____ o'clock.
3. _____.
4. _____.

**6** Listen and point. Ask your friends.

toast   jam   milk   cookies

cereal   orange juice   bread

| name | breakfast |
|---|---|
| Henry | milk and cookies |
| Hilary | toast and jam |
|  |  |
|  |  |

What do you have for breakfast?
Milk and cookies.

What do you have for breakfast?
Toast and jam.

What do you have for (breakfast)? (Toast) and (jam).

49

**7** Look and write.

Leo has breakfast at seven o'clock.
He eats _____ and he drinks _____.

Laura has _____.
She _____.

Tim _____.
_____.

He has (breakfast) at (seven) o'clock. He eats (toast).

**8** Sing the song.

Every Monday she eats cake,
She eats cake, she eats cake,
Every Monday she eats cake,
Every Monday.

Every Tuesday she drinks tea …

Every Wednesday she eats cheese …

Every Thursday she drinks milk …

Every Friday she eats fish …

Every Saturday she drinks juice …

Every Sunday she eats meat …

**9** Make a picture.

## My Portfolio

I have breakfast at eight o'clock.

I eat bread and jam. I drink milk.
Lena

I have (breakfast) at (seven) o'clock. I eat (toast).

51

# 5 The Red Parrot Club

**10**

**1** *A picnic in the woods …*
- It's one o'clock. I'm hungry.
- OK, let's eat. Mmm, I love pizza.

**2** *Suddenly …*
- Help! A monster!
- Run!

**3**
- What's the matter?
- There's a monster in the woods!
- It's enormous and it has brown hair.

**4**
- Come on. Let's find the monster.
- OK, Hayley!
- I have an idea.

**5**
- What's that?
- It's a monster trap.
- Good idea, Noah!

**6** "The monster's coming!"
"Quick, Noah! Hide!"

**7** "Oh, no!"

**8** "Aaaahhh!"
"That isn't a monster. It's Vinny!"

**9** "Where's Fay?"
"She's in your tree house. She's looking in the secret cupboard!"

**10** "Oh, no!" "The Super Shoes!"
"It's too late!"

# 5 Now I can...

**A** Write. Then choose, draw and write.

utaadysr    rafidy    yshrdatu    aewsenddy
ayusted    dunsay    yadmno

**Zabadoo's Super Sandwiches**

M o n d a y — cheese
T _ _ _ _ _ _ _ — sausage and tomato
W _ _ _ _ _ _ _ _ _ — chicken
T _ _ _ _ _ _ _ _ — cheese and tomato
F _ _ _ _ _ _ — jam
S _ _ _ _ _ _ _ _ — chicken and salad
S _ _ _ _ _ _ — jam and banana

Tuesday. Mmm. Sausage and tomato. My favorite! What's your favorite day?

_____. Mmm.
_____
_____.
My favorite!

**B** Can you look and write the times?

It's ten o'clock.

_____.

_____.

_____.

**C** Can you look and write?

On Monday, she has salad and oranges for lunch.
On Wednesday, _____.
_____.
_____.

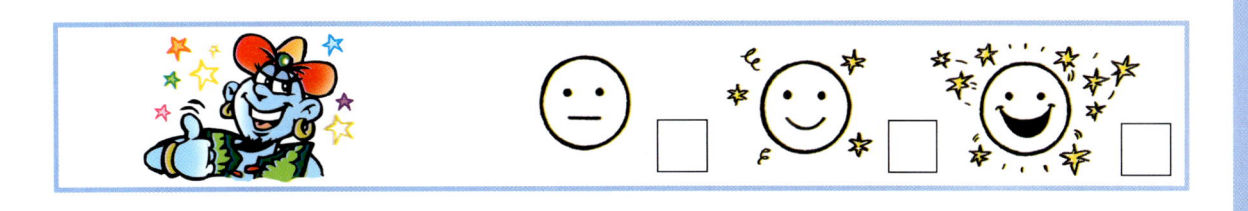

# The USA

**Culture Club**

The Grand Canyon

Canada

San Francisco

The West Coast

Pacific Ocean

Texas

Hollywood

Mexico

56

Golden Gate Bridge   film star   national park   cattle ranch

New York

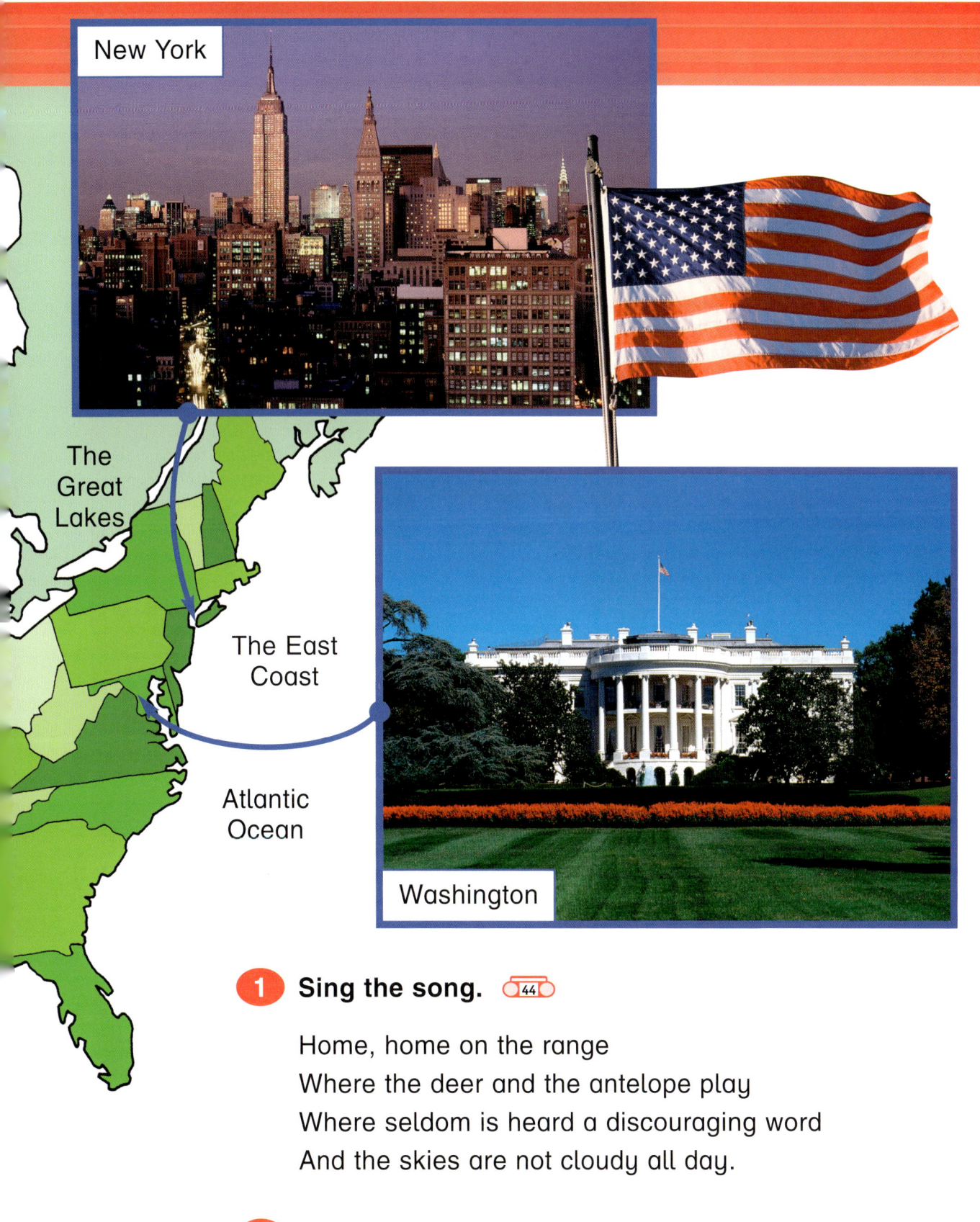

The Great Lakes

The East Coast

Atlantic Ocean

Washington

**1** **Sing the song.**

Home, home on the range
Where the deer and the antelope play
Where seldom is heard a discouraging word
And the skies are not cloudy all day.

**2** **Make a poster. 'Visit ...'**

skyscraper   capital   stars and stripes   The White House   ocean

57

# 6 Around town

**1** Listen and point. Listen and answer. 🔊 45

1. the bridge
2. the hotel
3. the train station
4. the bus station
5. the statue
6. the fountain

Where's the hotel?
It's opposite the bus station.

… behind …
… next to …
… in front of …

Where's the (fountain)? It's (next to) the bus station.

**2  Say the chant.** 🔊 46

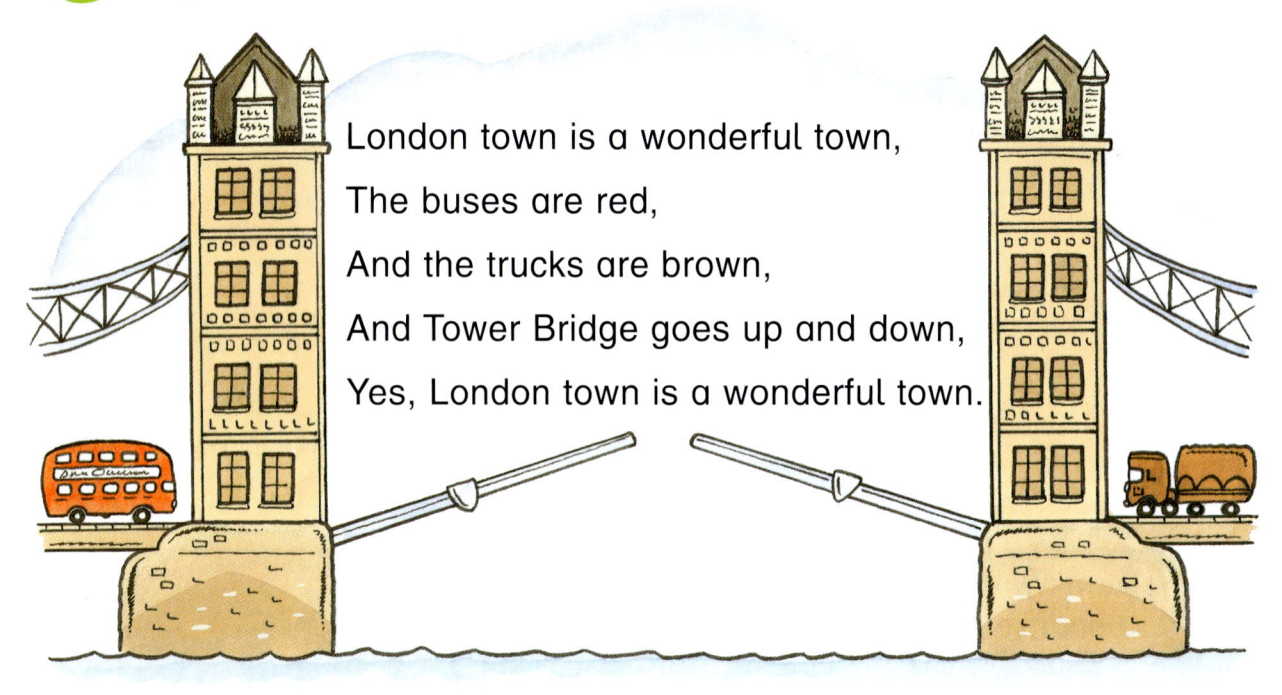

London town is a wonderful town,
The buses are red,
And the trucks are brown,
And Tower Bridge goes up and down,
Yes, London town is a wonderful town.

**3  Listen and follow.** 🔊 47

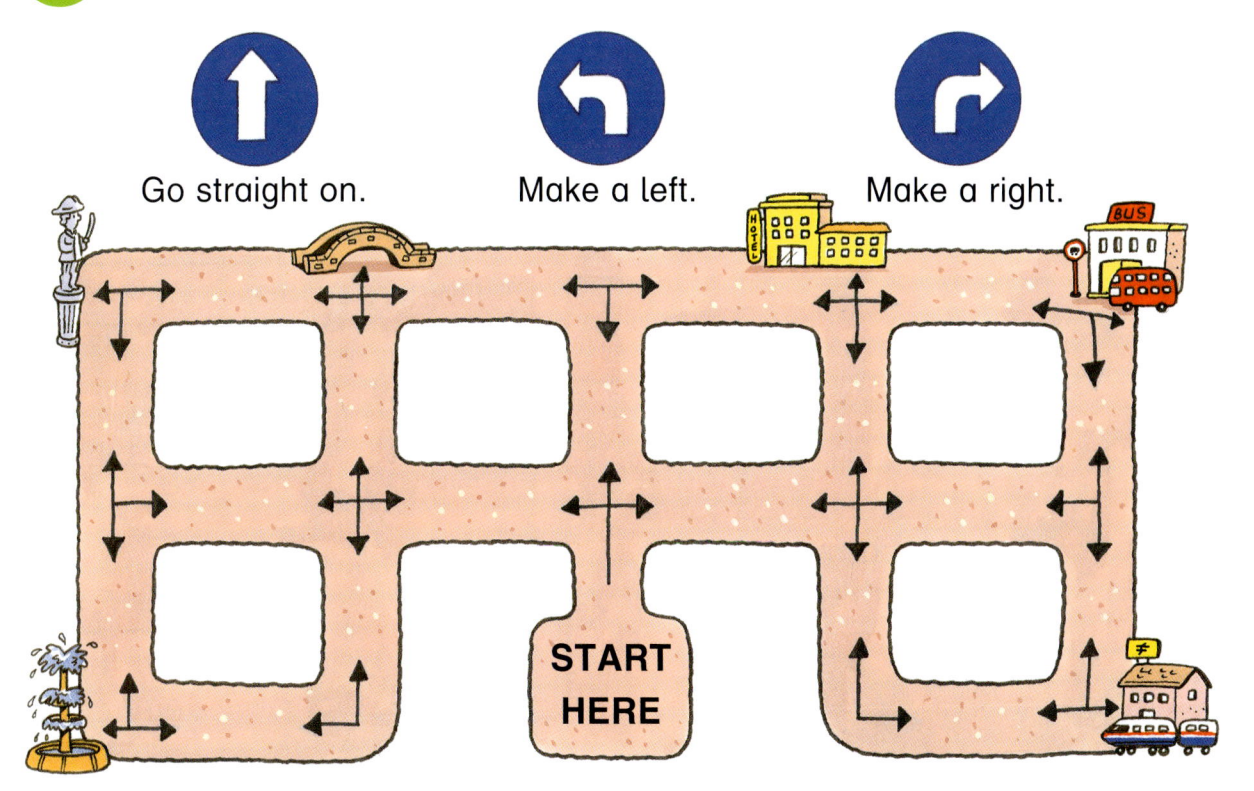

Go straight on.   Make a left.   Make a right.

START HERE

# 6 Where's the bus station?

**4** 🔊 48

**1** I'm late for my new job!

**2** Excuse me. Where's the bus station?
It's in Green Street. Go straight on. Make a right at the statue.

**3** Thank you! Goodbye!
Hmm. Where's the bus? It's late!

**4** At last! It's nine o'clock!

**5** A return ticket to Queen's Avenue, please.

**6** Where's Queen's Avenue?
Oh, no! It's you again!

**5** Listen and find the treasure. 🔊 49

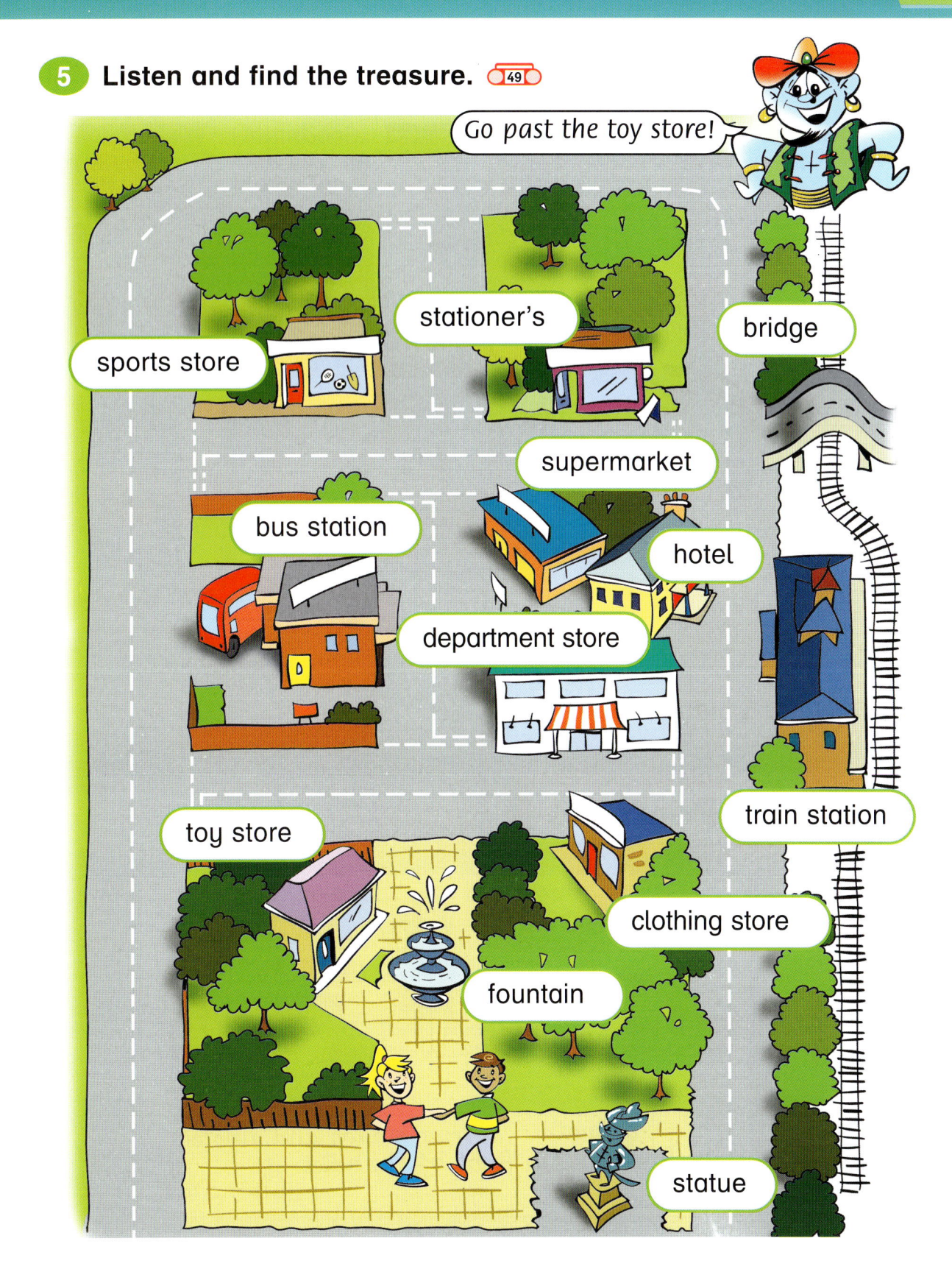

Go past the toy store!

sports store
stationer's
bridge
supermarket
bus station
hotel
department store
train station
toy store
clothing store
fountain
statue

**6** Listen, repeat and number.

a. See you later!

b. Goodnight!

c. Goodbye!

**7** Make a picture.

**My Portfolio**

My town

There's a fountain, a train station and a hotel. The fountain is in front of the hotel.

Chong Yew

**8  Sing the song.** 🔊 51

Oh, we're walking, walking, walking along,
Singing, singing, singing a song.
Zaba daba doo, zaba daba dee
Zaba daba doo, follow me!

Over the bridge and under the trees,
Look at the butterflies, look at the bees.
Hi, hi, hi, butterfly.
Zaba daba dee, bumblebee.

Make a right at the fountain,
Make a right at the fountain,
Don't stop at the fountain,
Go straight on, up the mountain.

Make a right at the fountain,
Make a right at the fountain,
Zaba daba doo, zaba daba dee
Zaba daba doo, follow me!

# The Red Parrot Club

**9** 🔊 52

**1** The Super Shoes aren't here.
Fay has them! Come on!

**2** In the town …
There's Fay. She's in front of the station.
And she's wearing the Super Shoes!

**3** She's escaping!
Let's catch her. Come on!

**4** Where is she, Mac? Can you see her?
Yes. She's behind the hotel. Make a right.

**5** Oh, no. There's Vinny, next to the fountain.
It's OK. I have an idea.

**6** What's that?

It's my new invention. Look, Fay's chasing Vinny!

**7** Fay! What are you doing? Stop!

I can't stop! Help!

**8** SPLASH!

Aaaahhh!

**9** Give me the Super Shoes.

Here you are. You can have them. I hate them!

**10** Where are we going?

I don't know. Let's find another adventure!

The End!

# 6

## Now I can...

**A** Can you do the puzzle?

1. s _ _ _ _ _ _
2. i _ _ _ _
3. e _ _ _ _ _ _ _
4. f _ _ _ _
5. f _ _ _ _ _ _
6. b _ _ _ _ _
7. z _ _ _ _
8. d _ _ _ _ _ _
9. l _ _ _
10. f _ _ _ _ _ _ _
11. t _ _
12. b _ _

**B** Can you color and write?

❶ = blue
❷ = red
❸ = green
❹ = yellow

The blue car *is in front of the hotel.*

The red car _____.

The green car _____.

The yellow car _____.

**C** Can you read and follow?

Make a right.
Make a left.
Make a right.

Where are you?
At the _____.

# Thanksgiving

**Culture Club**

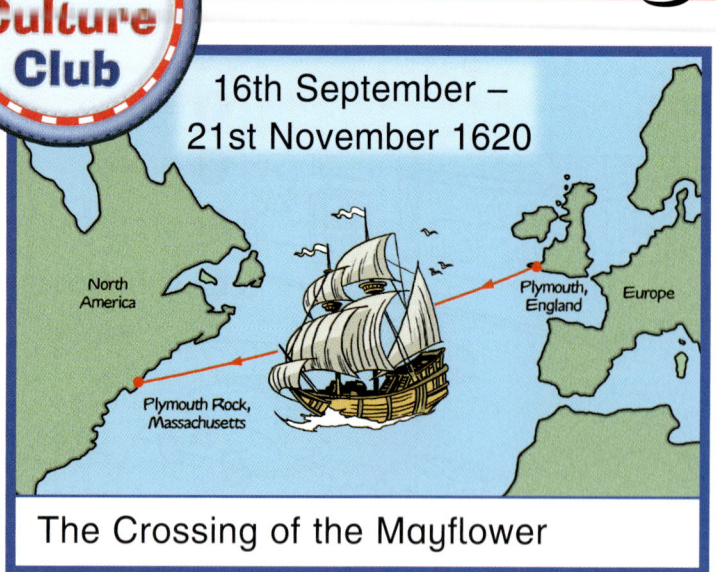

**16th September – 21st November 1620**

The Crossing of the Mayflower

The Wampanoag Indians

Thanksgiving is now a national holiday in the USA. Americans celebrate every year on the fourth Thursday in November.

turkey

pumpkin pie

ship   set sail   land   Fall

Fall (Autumn) 1621

The Plymouth Pilgrims

'Let us give thanks ...'

**1** **Make a 'tree of thanks'.**

**2** **Say the rhyme.**

The turkey is a funny bird.
Its head goes wobble, wobble.
And all it knows is just one word:
'Gobble, gobble, gobble!'

native Americans   Pilgrims   turkey   pumpkin pie

# Christmas

**Culture Club**

Roast turkey and Christmas pudding are the traditional dinner on Christmas Day. It is also traditional to make and decorate pies, cakes and cookies.

turkey    plum pudding    chocolate log

**1** **Make a Christingle.**

**2** **Sing the song.** 🔘55

Deck the halls with boughs of holly,
Fa la la la la, la la la la.
'Tis the season to be jolly,
Fa la la la la, la la la.

Sing we joyous, all together,
Fa la la la la la, la la la.
Heedless of the wind and weather,
Fa la la la la, la la la la.

cake   cookies   orange   candle

# Culture Club

# Valentine's Day

Saint Valentine is the patron saint of lovers. Valentine's Day is the 14th of February.

We write about 40 million cards and buy about 15 million red roses in the USA every year!

patron saint   mailbox   card   mailman

**1** Make a heart.

**2** Sing the song.

Oh my darling,
Oh my darling,
Oh my darling Valentine!
How I love you, more than ever.
I'll be yours, if you are mine.

red rose   chocolate   love   heart

# The Magic Piper

**Listen and act.** 🔊 57

**Scene 1**     This is the town of Hamelin. *The villagers have a problem.*
*There are animals everywhere! There is no food!*

| | |
|---|---|
| Villager 1 | Where's the milk? |
| Villager 2 | It's in the fridge. |
| Villagers 1 and 2 | Oh, no! A cat! |
| Villager 3 | Where's the cereal? |
| Villager 4 | It's in the cupboard. |
| Villagers 3 and 4 | Oh, no! A rabbit. |
| Villager 5 | Where's the bread? |
| Villager 6 | It's on the table. |
| Villagers 5 and 6 | Oh, no! A monkey. |
| Chorus 🎵 | *Monkeys swing, up and down* |

**Scene 2**     *The villagers go to see the king.*

| | |
|---|---|
| Villager 1 | Help us, please. There is no food. |
| King | Go away! I'm eating. |
| Chorus 🎵 | *Every Monday he eats cake* |
| Magic Piper | I can help you. I'm the Magic Piper. |
| Villager 2 | What can you do? |
| Magic Piper | I can take the animals away. |
| Villagers | Hurray! |
| King | OK. You can have 50 dollars. |
| Magic Piper | Thank you. Time for a spell! Animals, follow me! |
| Villagers | Hurray! |
| Chorus 🎵 | *Oh, we're walking along* |

74

**Scene 3**  	*Now there are no animals and the villagers are happy.*

Chorus 🎵  	*Every Monday we eat cake*
Villager 3  	Look! It's the Magic Piper.
Magic Piper  	Can I have 50 dollars, please?
King  	No! It's my money. Go away!
Magic Piper  	OK. Time for a spell! Children, follow me!
Villagers  	Oh, no!
Chorus 🎵  	*Oh, we're walking along*

**Scene 4**  	*Now there are no children and the villagers are sad.*

Chorus 🎵  	*Rainy, it's rainy, everyone is frowning*
Villager 4  	Where are the children?
Magic Piper  	It's a secret.
King  	Bring them back. Here's 50 dollars.
Magic Piper  	50 dollars? I want 100 dollars now!
King  	What a lot of money!
Villager 5  	Give him the money!
King  	Oh, OK. Here's 100 dollars.
Villagers  	10, 20, 30, 40, 50, 60, 70, 80, 90, 100!
Magic Piper  	Thank you. Time for a spell! Children, come home.
Chorus 🎵  	*Oh, we're walking along*
Villager 6  	Look! Our children! Hurray!
Chorus 🎵  	*Sunny, it's sunny, everyone is smiling*

# Picture Dictionary

**Look, write and stick.**

| UNIT 1 | UNIT 2 | UNIT 3 |
|---|---|---|

It's an e _ _ _ _ _ _ _ .

It's u _ _ _ _ the c _ _ _ _ .

It's w _ _ _ _ .

It's a f _ _ .

It's i _ the b _ _ _ .

It's c _ _ _ _ _ .

It's a z _ _ _ _ .

It's o _ the t _ _ _ _ .

It's s _ _ _ _ .

It's a m _ _ _ _ _ .

It's b _ _ _ _ _ the s _ _ _ .

It's r _ _ _ _ .

| UNIT 4 | UNIT 5 | UNIT 6 |
|---|---|---|
| It's a t _ _ store. | I love b _ _ _ _ _ _ _ _ ! | It's a b _ _ s _ _ _ _ _ _ . |
| It's a s _ _ _ _ _ _ _ _ _ _ . | I love l _ _ _ _ ! | It's a s _ _ _ _ _ . |
| It's a s _ _ _ _ _ store. | I love d _ _ _ _ _ ! | It's a b _ _ _ _ _ . |
| It's a p _ _ store. | I love s _ _ _ _ _ _ _ ! | It's a f _ _ _ _ _ _ _ _ . |

# Wordlist

## 1 Animals
all night a noite inteira
animal animal
arm braço
bite morder
crawl rastejar, arrastar
crocodile crocodilo
dolphin golfinho
Don't be silly! Não seja bobo!
elephant elefante
fast rapidamente
favorite preferido
fox raposa
fly voar
hop saltar
I can ... Eu posso ... Eu sei....
leg perna
letter carta
like como
lion leão
monkey macaco
mouse ratinho
short curto
small pequeno
swim nadar
swing balançar
tail cauda
tiger tigre
walk caminhar/andar
wing asa
zebra zebra

### Culture Club: Pets
cage gaiola
cat gato
dog cachorro
collar coleira
fish peixe
hamster hamster
parrot papagaio
pet animal de estimação
rabbit coelho
survey pesquisa

## 2 Our house
bath banheira
Be careful! Cuidado!
bed cama
behind atrás
bedroom quarto
blond louro
bookcase estante
chair cadeira
cupboard armário
Do you know? Você sabe/conhece?
fridge geladeira
Glove luva
hair cabelos
I don't know. Eu não sei. Eu não conheço

igloo iglu
mice ratinhos
on sobre
open aberto
other outro
sky céu
sofa sofá
stove fogão
table mesa
There are ... Há, Existem ...
There's/There is ... Há, Existe...
tree house casa da árvore
want querer
What's happening? O que está acontecendo?
Where do you live? Onde você mora?
Why? Por quê?

## 3 In the park
box caixa
dance dançar
drink beber
frown levantar as sobrancelhas
glad contente, feliz
It's cloudy. Está nublado.
It's rainy. Está chovendo.
It's snowy. Está nevando.
It's sunny. Faz sol.
It's windy. Está ventando.
knit tricotar
lie deitar
play (tennis) jogar (tênis)
play (the guitar) tocar (violão)
sad triste
skate andar de patins
smile sorrir
trumpet trompete
What's he doing? O que ele está fazendo?
What's the weather like? Como está o tempo?

### Culture Club: Home
cabin cabana
carpet tapete
fireplace lareira
front door porta de entrada
garage garagem
porch varanda
roof telhado
window janela
yard quintal

## 4 Shopping
bear urso
buy comprar
Can I borrow...? Você me empresta ...?
computer computador
curly hair cabelos cacheados
cheese queijo
doll boneca

dollar dólar
eighty oitenta
honey pot pote de mel
How much is/are ...? Quanto custa/custam ...?
hundred cem
magazine revista
money dinheiro
ninety noventa
puppet marionete
secret segredo
seventy setenta
shop loja
shopping mall shopping center
sixty sessenta
something algo, alguma coisa
stationer's papelaria
supermarket supermercado
sweet bala
warm quente
webcam webcam
What a lot of money! Quanto dinheiro!

## 5 Meal times
bad mal
banana banana
breakfast café da manhã
bread pão
cake bolo
carrot cenoura
cereal cereais
chips batatinhas
cookies biscoitos
dinner jantar
enormous enorme
feed alimentar
Friday sexta-feira
have breakfast tomar café da manhã
It's eight o'clock. São oito horas.
jam geléia
juice suco
lunch almoço
milk leite
Monday segunda-feira
monster monstro
orange laranja
pea ervilha
salad salada
Saturday sábado
sausage salsicha
Sunday domingo
tea chá
Thursday quinta-feira
toast torrada
tomato tomate
trap armadilha
Tuesday terça-feira
Wednesday quarta-feira
What time is it? Que horas são?

### Culture Club: The USA
capital capital
cattle ranch fazenda de gado
film star estrela de cinema
national park parque nacional
ocean oceano
skyscraper arrantha-céu
stars and stripes estrelas e listras
The White House A Casa Branca

### 6 Around town
adventure aventura
at last finalmente
bee abelha
bumblebee abelhinha
bridge ponte
bus ônibus
butterfly borboleta
department store loja de departamento
Excuse me. Com licença.
follow seguir
fountain fonte
Go straight on. Siga em frente.
hotel hotel
in front of em frente a
invention invenção
job trabalho
next to ao lado de
opposite em frente a
over sobre
past passando, depois de
return ticket bilhete de ida e volta
See you later! Até mais tarde
station estação
statue estátua
tower torre
train trem
treasure tesouro
truck caminhão
Make a left. Vire à esquerda.
Make a right. Vire à direita.
wonderful maravilhoso

### Culture Club: Thanksgiving
Fall outono
land terra
native Americans índios americanos
pilgrims peregrinos
pumpkin pie torta de abóbora
set sail leventar as velas/velejar
ship navio
turkey peru

### Culture Club: Christmas
body corpo
chocolate log bolo de chocolate em forma de tronco
Christmas Day Dia de Natal
hang pendurar
holly sagrado
pie torta
pudding pudim
snowman boneco de neve
stocking meia
turkey peru

### Culture Club: Valentine's day
card cartão
chocolate log torta de chocolate
heart coracão
love amor, amar
mailbox caixa do correio
mailman carteiro
patron saint santo padroeiro
red rose rosa vermelha

### The Magic Piper
bring back trazer de volta
magic piper flautista mágico
take away levar embora

# OXFORD
UNIVERSITY PRESS

Great Clarendon Street, Oxford OX2 6DP

Oxford University Press is a department of the University of Oxford.
It furthers the University's objective of excellence in research, scholarship,
and education by publishing worldwide in

Oxford  New York

Auckland  Cape Town  Dar es Salaam  Hong Kong  Karachi
Kuala Lumpur  Madrid  Melbourne  Mexico City  Nairobi
New Delhi  Shanghai  Taipei  Toronto

With offices in

Argentina  Austria  Brazil  Chile  Czech Republic  France  Greece
Guatemala  Hungary  Italy  Japan  Poland  Portugal  Singapore
South Korea  Switzerland  Thailand  Turkey  Ukraine  Vietnam

OXFORD and OXFORD ENGLISH are registered trade marks of
Oxford University Press in the UK and in certain other countries

© Oxford University Press 2005

The moral rights of the author have been asserted

Database right Oxford University Press (maker)

First published 2005

2016  2015  2014  2013  2012
10 9

**No unauthorized photocopying**

All rights reserved. No part of this publication may be reproduced,
stored in a retrieval system, or transmitted, in any form or by any means,
without the prior permission in writing of Oxford University Press,
or as expressly permitted by law, or under terms agreed with the appropriate
reprographics rights organization. Enquiries concerning reproduction
outside the scope of the above should be sent to the ELT Rights Department,
Oxford University Press, at the address above

You must not circulate this book in any other binding or cover
and you must impose this same condition on any acquirer

Any websites referred to in this publication are in the public domain and
their addresses are provided by Oxford University Press for information only.
Oxford University Press disclaims any responsibility for the content

ISBN: 978 0 19 477311 9

Printed in China

ACKNOWLEDGEMENTS

*Illustrations by:* Nick Diggory, Zabadoo artwork; Gavin Reece, The Red Parrot Club comic strip; Alan Rowe, Hilary and Henry wizard artwork; Kathy Baxendale pp 6, 12, 13, 19, 29, 40, 62; Garry Davies pp 3, 5, 10, 11, 23, 33, 39, 44, 45, 59, 66; Kelly Harrison p 51; John Haslam: sticker artwork; Andy Hunt pp 28, 41; Kevin Hopgood pp 68, 69; Claire Mumford pp 7, 63; Chris Pavely pp 56, 57, 69; Adam Stower pp 18, 74, 75.

*Commissioned photography by:* Gareth Boden pp 12 (hamster cage) 69, 70 (Christmas food), 71 (Christingle); 72, 73; Mark Mason pp 37, 40;

*The Publishers would like to thank the following for their kind permission to reproduce photographs and other copyright material:* Alamy Images pp 35 (bathroom/Elizabeth Whiting & Associates, bedroom/Abode Interiors Picture Library, log cabin/MedioImages), 56 (Grand Canyon/GP Bowater, San Francisco/K-Photos, Hollywood sign/ImageState), 57 (White House/PCL); Corbis pp 57 (New York/Richard Berenholtz), 68 (Thanksgiving dinner/Larry Williams), 72 (mailbox/Chase Swift, mailman/Cathrine Wessel); DK Images p 13 (rabbit/Mike Dunning); Getty Images pp 12 (cat in tree/John Livzey/ Stone, dog/Eric Pearle/Photographer's Choice); OUP pp 56 (cowboys/Brand X Pictures), 57 (USA flag/Image Farm Inc.), 71 (holly/Brand X Pictures), 72 (calendar, rose/Photodisc, chocolate box/Ingram, heart shaped balloon/ Comstock), 73 (hearts/Image Source); Photolibrary.com p68 (pumpkin pie/Foodpix); Punchstock pp 34 (house/Digital Vision), 35 (lounge/Brand X Pictures).

*Cover photography:* Group of children/Photodisc.

# Kids United

Livro de Atividades **4**

OXFORD

**OXFORD**
UNIVERSITY PRESS

Great Clarendon Street, Oxford OX2 6DP UK

Oxford University Press is a department of the University of Oxford.
It furthers the University's objective of excellence in research, scholarship,
and education by publishing worldwide in

Oxford New York

Auckland Cape Town Dar es Salaam Hong Kong Karachi
Kuala Lumpur Madrid Melbourne Mexico City Nairobi
New Delhi Shanghai Taipei Toronto

With offices in

Argentina Austria Brazil Chile Czech Republic France Greece
Guatemala Hungary Italy Japan Poland Portugal Singapore
South Korea Switzerland Thailand Turkey Ukraine Vietnam

OXFORD and OXFORD ENGLISH are registered trademarks of
Oxford University Press

© 2008 Oxford University Press

The moral rights of the author have been asserted

Database right Oxford University Press (maker)

First published 2008

2012, 2011, 2010, 2009, 2008

10 9 8 7 6 5 4 3 2 1

All rights reserved. No part of this publication may be reproduced,
stored in a retrieval system, or transmitted, in any form or by any means,
without the prior permission in writing of Oxford University Press (with
the sole exception of photocopying carried out under the conditions stated
in the paragraph headed 'Photocopying'), or as expressly permitted by law, or
under terms agreed with the appropriate reprographics rights organization.
Enquiries concerning reproduction outside the scope of the above should
be sent to the ELT Rights Department, Oxford University Press, at the
address above

You must not circulate this book in any other binding or cover
and you must impose this same condition on any acquirer

**Photocopying**

The Publisher grants permission for the photocopying of those pages marked
'photocopiable' according to the following conditions. Individual purchasers
may make copies for their own use or for use by classes that they teach. School
purchasers may make copies for use by staff and students, but this permission
does not extend to additional schools or branches

Under no circumstances may any part of this book be photocopied for resale

Any websites referred to in this publication are in the public domain and their
addresses are provided by Oxford University Press for information only. Oxford
University Press disclaims any responsibility for the content

Editor: Ana Lúcia Militello
Designer: Marília Garcia
Illustrated by: Nick Diggory

978 000040132 8

Printed in Brazil.

# KIDS UNITED

Livro de Atividades 4

| Índice | Página |
|---|---|
| Unidade 1 | 4 |
| Unidade 2 | 6 |
| Unidade 3 | 8 |
| Unidade 4 | 10 |
| Unidade 5 | 12 |
| Unidade 6 | 14 |

OXFORD

# Animals

## A - Complete the words.

## B - Match. Write sentences.

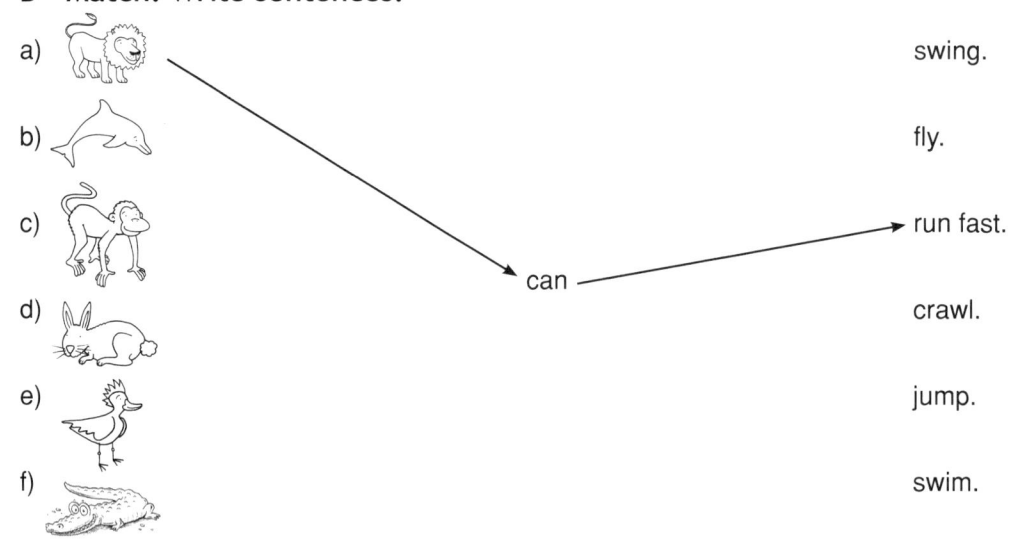

a) swing.
b) fly.
c) run fast.
   can
d) crawl.
e) jump.
f) swim.

Example: a) A lion can run fast.
b) _____
c) _____
d) _____
e) _____
f) _____

C - Read and complete the text.

> IS   HAS   CAN

This is my pet. It _is_ brown.

It _____ small ears and a long tail.

It _____ walk and run. It can swing, too.

It _____ up that tree... Look!

D - Draw the pet according to the text in exercise 3.

# 2 Our house

A - Read. Write the room in a house.

a) A sofa, a chair, a small table and television. _____

b) A bath, a toilet and a sink. _____

c) A cupboard, a table, a stove and a fridge. _____

d) A table, a chair and one bed. _____

B - Match the objects to the rooms in the house.

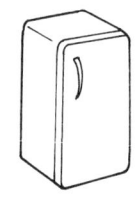

the bedroom          the bathroom

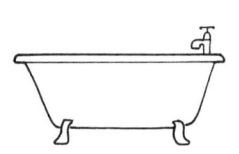

the living room   the dining room   the kitchen

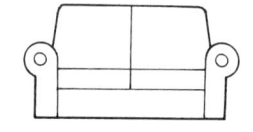

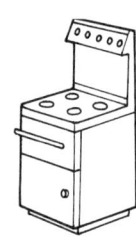

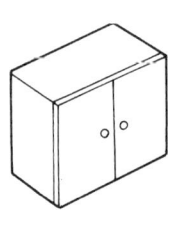

Unidade 2

## C - Read and complete with: *There is / There are*.

My bedroom is cool. _____ one for me, and one for my sister. _____ a          and a       . _____ a             under the window. _____             and           in the bookcase. _____ a          under my bed and _____         ,         , and a       under my sister's bed.

## B - Match.

a) There is a cat under the box.

b) There is a cat behind the box.

c) There is a cat in the box.

d) There is a cat on the box.

Unidade 2

# 3 In the park

**A - Look and complete the action.**

_____ water.

_____ an ice cream.

_____ a song.

_____ a bike.

_____ tennis.

_____ soccer.

**B - Look at the pictures. Circle true or false.**

There is a girl riding a bike. TRUE / FALSE

There is a boy skating in the park. TRUE / FALSE

There is a girl eating. TRUE / FALSE

There is a boy drinking Coke. TRUE / FALSE

There is a girl playing tennis. TRUE / FALSE

There is a dog running. TRUE / FALSE

Unidade 3

C - Read and match.

It's sunny.   It's cloudy.   It's rainy.   It's windy.

D - Describe what the kids are doing.

1)  2)  3) 
4)  5)  6)

1) She's walking.
2) _____.
3) _____.
4) _____.
5) _____.
6) _____.

# 4 Shopping

**A - Match the name of the place.**

1) Where can you buy soccer balls, tennis rackets and sports uniforms?

2) Where can you buy games, skateboards, kites and dolls?

3) Where can you buy rulers, pencil cases, pencils and pens?

4) Where can you buy food and juice?

5) Where can you buy food for pets?

6) Where can you buy socks, jeans and T-shirts?

STATIONER'S
THE PET SHOP
THE CLOTING STORE
THE TOY STORE
THE SUPERMARKET
The Sports Store

**B - Write.** *How much is it?*

1) 10.40    2) 2    3) 2.10    4) 3.65

1) _____  2) _____  3) _____  4) _____

Unidade 4

C - Read and complete the dialogue.

| sorry | How much | Thanks | loves | have | Five | flowers |

Let's buy some _____ for your mom.

OK. I _____ $ 4.

_____ are these flowers?

_____ dollars.

Those flowers are $4.50.

Can I borrow 50 cents, please, Laura?

Of course. Here you are, Leo.

_____.

My mom _____ pink flowers.

My hat! Please, be careful!

_____, Mrs. Sharp!

D - Read.

> I want to buy presents for my family!
> I want to buy a dog in the clothing store for my baby sister.
> For my brothers, I want to buy a soccer ball in the stationer's.
> I want to buy a red pen for Mom and a calculator for Dad in the sports store.
> For me, a blue and green jacket from the pet store.
> Yes, perfect! Er…. Now,
> I want money for the presents…

**Now, write the text correcting the name of the places.**

Unidade 4

# 5 Meal times

**A - Complete the puzzle.**

**D
E
L
I
C
I
O
U
S**

**B - Look and find. Write.**

MON ___ ___ ___    TUE ___ ___ ___ ___    WED ___ ___ ___ ___ ___ ___

THU ___ ___ ___ ___ ___    FRI ___ ___ ___

What are the days of the weekend? ___ ___ ___ ___ ___ ___ ___ ___ and

___ ___ ___ ___ ___ ___

| S | D | W | E | D | N | E | S | D | A | Y |
|---|---|---|---|---|---|---|---|---|---|---|
| A | O | T | H | U | R | S | D | A | Y | E |
| T | U | E | S | D | A | Y | G | M | M | S |
| U | M | R | U | S | R | D | H | U | O | F |
| R | A | D | N | D | F | N | J | N | N | E |
| D | N | U | D | E | R | E | K | Q | D | R |
| A | P | Y | A | Y | Y | U | A | E | A | D |
| Y | R | G | Y | F | R | I | D | A | Y | I |

What day of the week is it today? _____

Unidade 5

**C - Write sentences.**

1) [likes] [fish] [Mark]
   _____.

2) [chicken] [Paula] [likes]
   _____.

3) [Leo] [for breakfast] [orange juice] [likes]
   _____.

4) [doesn't] [Dad] [sausages] [like]
   _____.

5) [Sandy] [Leo] [and] [carrots] [love]
   _____.

**D - Read the sentences in exercise C. Answer *YES* or *NO***

1) Does Leo like orange juice for breakfast? _____

2) Does Mark like fish? _____

3) Does Paula like chicken? _____

4) Does Paula like carrots? _____

# Around town

**A - Match the directions.**

Make a right.          Make a left.          Go straight on.

**B - Match.**

1) At           late.
2) Make         straight on.
3) Thank        me.
4) Excuse       a left.
5) I'm          last.
6) Go           you.

**C - Answer the questions.**

1) What's the day today?

_____

2) What's the weather like today?

_____

3) What time do you have lunch?

_____

4) How much is a sandwich and a juice?

_____

5) What do you have for breakfast?

_____

D - Look at the map and answer.

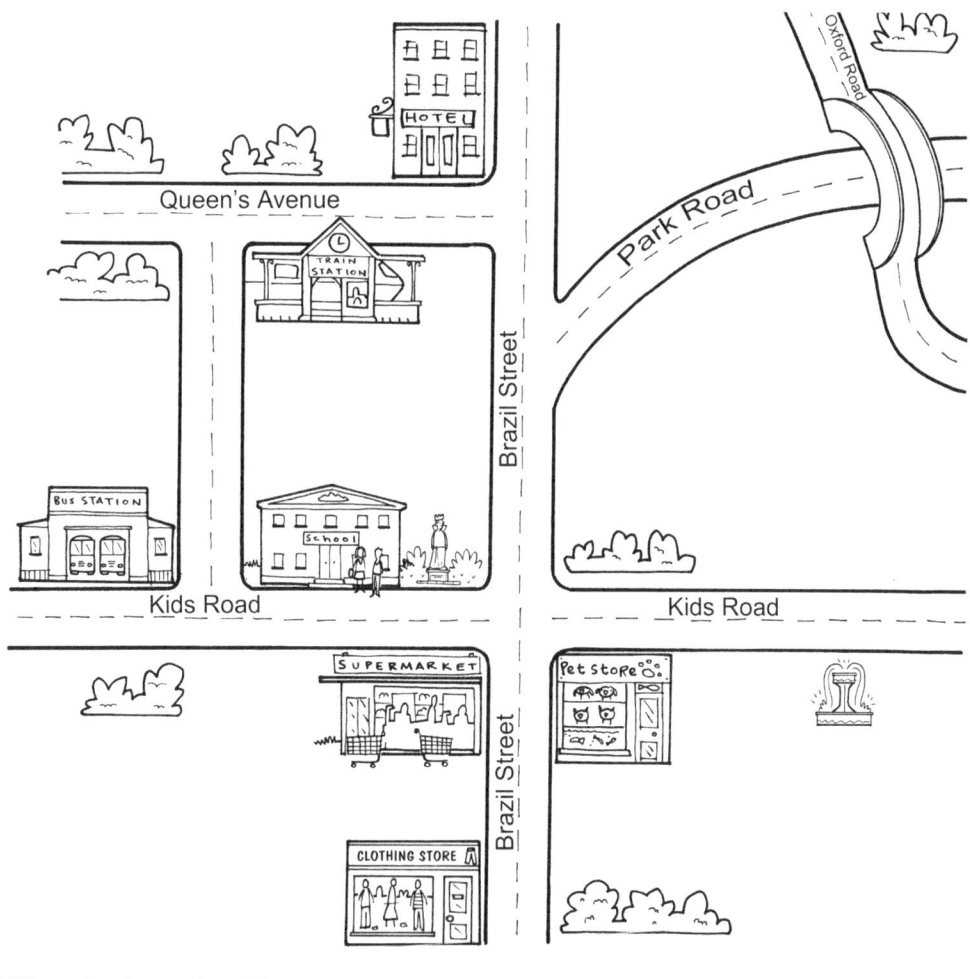

1) Where's the school? _____

2) Where's the statue? _____

3) Where's the pet store? _____

4) Where's the clothing store? _____

E - Look at the map and answer the questions in exercise C.

1) <u>There is a fountain in the park.</u>

_____

_____

_____

Unidade 6

# KIDS UNITED

**KIDS UNITED** é a mais nova coleção de inglês americano em 5 volumes para crianças a partir de seis anos.

**KIDS UNITED** combina personagens cativantes, músicas variadas e atividades lúdicas diversificadas para que a criança seja envolvida de forma prazerosa no processo de aprendizado.

E mais:
- Atividades de personalização ao final de cada unidade.
- Histórias em quadrinhos estimulam e motivam a leitura.
- Seção *Culture Club* - ideal para trabalhar a interdisciplinaridade e Temas Transversais.
- Livro do professor em português.
- *Portfolio & Test and Evaluation Booklet* - Livreto com testes e atividades extras fotocopiáveis para completar o Portfolio dos alunos.
- www.oup.com/elt/kidsunitedbrazil - oferece jogos e exercícios interativos para o aluno.
- www.oup.com/elt/teacher/kidsunitedbrazil - com sugestões de atividades extras para o professor.

OXFORD 000040132-3

9 780000 401328

**OXFORD**
UNIVERSITY PRESS

www.oup.com/elt